WEATHER OR NOT...

IT'S A CLIMATE FOR CHANGE

by Caren Trafford

Illustrations by David Wilsher

MEET THE WEATHER-MAKERS

MUZBAR – well known intergalactic weather detective. Since Pluto has been down-graded to a dwarf planet, Muzbar is on a new mission – to seek out ways to down-grade global warming alerts on Earth.

STORM FRONT AND THE WEATHER VANES – top sellers in the weather charts. Famous for kicking up a storm. Their fans always look up at them.

SOUWESTER – a colourful wet-weather gal. Likes sailors, traders and all kinds of wind-bags.

THE GHG GANG – they pack a powerful punch when heated. If you don't play clean... they get mean.

WEATHER-POD – resident weather guru, who believes that most weather is just a front and it's time to download the facts.

POO-LOOTER – a bit of an old fossil who likes heating things up. Time to send him on a well earned holiday.

etram

Published by Etram Pty Ltd
www.planetkids.biz

First published in Australia 2007
3rd edition 2007

National Library of Australia
Cataloguing-in-Publisher entry :
Trafford, Caren
Weather or Not...
it's a Climate for Change
ISBN 0-9581878-3-5

Illustrator: David Wilsher
Design: Bernadette Gethings
Printed in China through Bookbuilders

WEATHER ... LOVES TO BE THE CENTRE OF ATTENTION.

Like a movie star, it gets discussed for hours. What is it up to? What will it do next?

Some like it hot... others cold. People compare yesterday's weather with last year's; complain about the rain, or how to beat the heat. Either it's too wet or too dry. What will it be like tomorrow?

Weather is possibly the most talked about topic on this planet. So why, if weather is so popular, isn't anyone looking after it?

I'm Muzbar, intergalactic weather detective. Together with my partners, Storm Front and Weather-Pod, we're busy tracking the gossip.

News is pouring in and we're snowed under by all the facts. No, we haven't been sitting out in the sun too long without a hat and we didn't come down with the last drop of rain.

We've dried out the myths, kicked up a storm and blown off the wind to reveal the hot truth. The forecast is...

Keep an umbrella handy - you never know what's about to come down

Come rain, wind or shine, YOU can make a big difference to the weather and climate over the next 10, 50, 100 years, whether you like it or not...

THAT'S A WRAP

Time to uncover the BIG picture.

Wrapped around this planet is a cloak of invisible gas called the atmosphere. You can't see, smell or touch it, but like a gi-normous security blanket it's out there protecting the Earth.

Thanks to the atmosphere, Earth is shielded from the sun's heat, safe-guarded from harmful radiation and insulated from freezing.

Kept in place by gravity, the atmosphere helps to control weather and climate. Without it, temperatures everywhere would be horridly hot during the day and flipping freezing at night. *You'd need to stay indoors most of the time!*

Share a blanket. It's a great way to make friends

This blanket of invisible gas also protects Earth from space invaders; burning up millions of tiny and not-so-tiny meteors whenever they stray too close. Thickest at the Earth's surface, the atmosphere thins down to just a dribble as it spreads out, eventually merging into the vacuum of space. Other planets also have atmospheres, but Earth's is special: it contains water and oxygen.

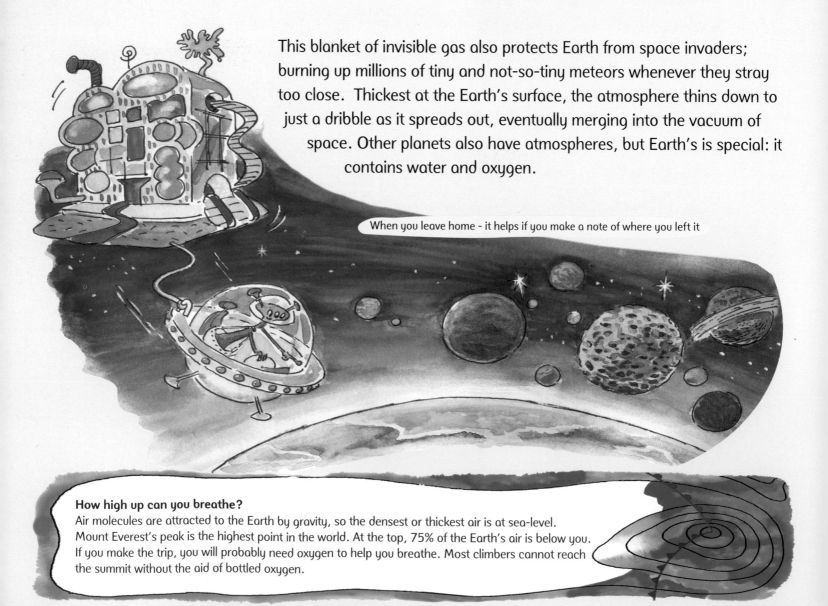

When you leave home - it helps if you make a note of where you left it

How high up can you breathe?
Air molecules are attracted to the Earth by gravity, so the densest or thickest air is at sea-level. Mount Everest's peak is the highest point in the world. At the top, 75% of the Earth's air is below you. If you make the trip, you will probably need oxygen to help you breathe. Most climbers cannot reach the summit without the aid of bottled oxygen.

THE MAGIC FORMULA

What is in the Earth's atmosphere?

Take 75% nitrogen, some oxygen and a pinch (less than one percent) of argon. Mix it all together and you will create a giant life-giving ocean of air.

But there's more! The rest of the atmosphere - *less than 0.05 percent* – contains the magic mix for life on Earth.

What are the secret ingredients?

Firstly, there's a thin layer of Ozone gas which forms a protective barrier against the sun's fierce radiation.

Secondly, a very special mix of naturally-occurring Greenhouse gases, (*we call them the GHG gang*), stops the planet from freezing. Without them, you'd be living on a frozen rock, *like Mars.*

Recipes work best if you start off with the right ingredients

LIVING UNDER PRESSURE

The atmosphere is not the same the whole way through. It's made up of five layers, each with a different temperature. As you move upwards through each layer, the atmospheric pressure or amount of air decreases. What you call every-day weather occurs in the lowest level of the atmosphere. Can you feel the air pressure around you? *It's roughly equal to the force of an elephant balancing on a desk!*

The three global temperature measurements	Kelvin	Celsius	Fahrenheit
Absolute zero	0 K	−273°C	−460°F
Melting point of ice	273 K	0°C	32°F
Water's boiling point	373 K	100°C	212°F

Exosphere
Top Floor - Penthouse
500 km above the Earth, the atmosphere merges into space. Satellites orbit in this layer - 500 km to 1,000 km from Earth.

Thermosphere
Getting Cooler
A thin ribbon of gas between 80 km and 110 km up. Space shuttle territory and home to the Aurora Lights – bands of coloured light, caused as the sun's rays pass through the atmospheric gases above the Poles.

Mesosphere
Going Up
The coldest part of the atmosphere, 50-80 km above Earth. Meteors burn up in this layer.

Stratosphere
Great View
It gets warmer here - 30 to km up. Home to the Ozone layer and fierce winds that circle the planet.

Troposphere
Ground Floor
From the surface up to 15 km. This is the only breathable part of the atmosphere; warmest at the bottom and coolest at the top. Also, this is the only area where air between the Northern and Southern hemispheres hardly mixes, so the more polluted air from the crowded Northern hemisphere does not spread to people living south of the Equator. *Southerners make their own pollution!*

Tropopause
separates the troposphere from the next layer. The two together are called the lower atmosphere.

What goes up doesn't always come down

PUTTING THE PIECES TOGETHER

Weather is like a gigantic puzzle. You need to fit all the pieces together to see the big picture!

The main puzzle pieces are, heat from the sun, the movement of massive amounts of air and moisture, gravity's pull and a planet spinning on a tilted axis.

As the Earth orbits the sun, the part tilted closest to the sun gets hotter. Land areas and continents absorb heat more quickly than oceans, so world-wide there are big temperature differences. The hottest temperature on record is about 58°C, while the coldest is a very chilly minus 90°C.

The Earth spins at an angle of 23.5 degrees, so why doesn't everyone fall off? *Gravity* – it's always trying to hold you down and most importantly, it stops the planet's air from just flying off into space.

Heat can't bear to stand still, so Nature tries to reduce the temperature differences by using gravity. Warm air is lighter than cold air. As it rises, the heavier cold air flows into the space left behind by the warmer air.

The Equator being nearer the sun… *it sticks out more*… receives more heat than either the North or South Poles. Air over land heats and rises up faster than the air over water, creating more temperature differences that gravity tries to balance out.

Vast air masses with very different temperatures occur all around the planet, creating huge swirls of warm and cold air, 1,000s of kilometres wide. Known as low and high pressure systems, these produce the weather changes.

In weather-speak, high air-pressure is associated with sunny conditions and clear skies. Low air pressure usually means clouds, storms and unsettled weather.

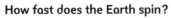

How fast does the Earth spin?
If you're standing at the North Pole, the speed is almost zero but at the Equator, where the circumference of Earth is greatest, the speed is about 1,670 kilometres per hour.

POWER TO THE WATER

The Water Cycle also plays an important part in the weather puzzle.

The sun heats up water changing it to vapour.

90% of the moisture in the atmosphere is water that has evaporated from the oceans. The rest evaporates from rivers, lakes and even plants and animals.

Getting around is easier with the right ticket

Water vapour rises and meets the cooler air higher up, where it condenses and re-forms as moisture in clouds. Depending on temperatures, wind currents and land shapes, this moisture eventually falls back to earth. About 75% falls into the sea as rain and snow. The rest falls on land and flows down to rivers or seeps into underground streams, eventually finding its way back to the sea. So, the water cycle continues.

Is there heat on the streets?
Warm air can hold more moisture than cold air. That means your washing dries more quickly if it is hung out to dry on a warm day.

ENERGY REMOVALISTS

Ocean currents are another piece of the weather puzzle. 70% of the Earth's surface is covered by oceans that act as gigantic solar collectors, trapping heat from the sun. Did you know that the average depth of the ocean is 1,000 metres? How much water is that?

Water currents flow throughout the oceans like fast moving rivers. Imagine a huge conveyor belt able to transfer enormous quantities of water, heat and energy from one place to another. That's what currents do.

Helped by a global network of winds, currents move warm and cold water around the planet; from the Equator towards the icy regions at the North and South Poles, changing the weather patterns of the countries they pass.

If you fancy a free ride, join a current movement

The Gulf Stream and the North Atlantic Drift are two currents that control the climate of Northern Europe. Carrying warm water from the Gulf of Mexico and the Caribbean across the Atlantic to Europe, they deliver the same amount of heat as one million power stations, heating up temperatures in some regions by 10°C.

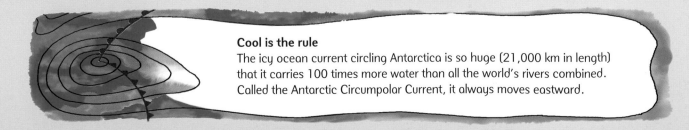

Cool is the rule
The icy ocean current circling Antarctica is so huge (21,000 km in length) that it carries 100 times more water than all the world's rivers combined. Called the Antarctic Circumpolar Current, it always moves eastward.

IT'S ONLY A PUDDLE

Together, the sun, water, air and currents create a global heat engine that pumps out the weather.

The Earth's spin is the final part of the puzzle. The spin pushes air at the Equator in an easterly direction. That's why weather systems generally move from west to east.

Strong westward Trade Winds near South America keep Peru's coastal waters at a lower level than those on the opposite side of the Pacific. Every two to seven years, these powerful winds relax, allowing a huge warm water mass – *roughly the size of Europe* – to move back east across the Pacific; like warm water swirling in a giant bathtub.

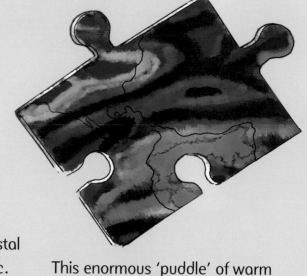

This enormous 'puddle' of warm water is called *El Niño*. Containing a huge amount of energy, it changes weather patterns and turns the world's weather-machine topsy-turvy.

Sometimes, even the weather gets into hot water

For people living in Indonesia, Australia or southern Africa, *El Niño* means hotter weather, droughts and forest fires. On the other side of the Pacific, South Americans associate *El Niño* with rainstorms, floods and mudslides. *That's one powerful puddle.*

Fancy a break?
High up in the sky, winds blow mainly from west to east. If you fly from Europe to Australia your plane will arrive one hour quicker because the wind is behind you. It will take an hour longer on the way back, because you're flying into the wind. *So, if you want to start your holiday one hour earlier... fly east!*

12

WHO'S GOT WIND?

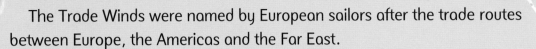

Meet Souwester. What a colourful character – and guess from which direction she blows? Here's a hint… winds are named after where they come from, not where they blow to.

The Trade Winds were named by European sailors after the trade routes between Europe, the Americas and the Far East.

When Dutch sailors began trading with the Spice Islands, their merchant ships battled the seas and fierce gales at latitudes 40° and 50° south. These winds were named, the *Roaring Forties, Furious Fifties* and *Screaming Sixties.* Some of the strongest winds rage around the Screaming Sixties – *fancy some kite-flying?*

Monsoons blow at certain times of the year. The name comes from the word, *mausim* meaning season. Tornadoes are named after the Spanish word *tornare*, meaning 'to turn'.

Have you seen a *Willy Willy* or a *Dust Devil? They like to get around.*

The Doctor and the *Southerly Buster* are on-shore winds that bust the heat and make you feel better.

Jet Streams are long and narrow *streams* of wind that blow at high altitudes. They were named during World War II when pilots found that their speed decreased if they flew against them. Birds have the right idea. They catch the jet streams when they migrate. *It's a great free ride, so long as you're going in the right direction.*

Hurricanes are the strongest of all wild weather wind warnings. In Antarctica, wind speeds can reach 320 kilometres per hour.

How are hurricanes named? **The World Meteorological Organisation** chooses names using each letter of the alphabet starting from 'A'. Six lists are used in rotation. When a hurricane is very deadly, or costly, the original name is taken off the list and a new name is added.

It's hot in the pot
Bar-headed geese, the world's highest-altitude migrant birds, fly each year to nesting grounds in Tibet. With a little help from the jet-streams, they can cover the one-way trip; more than 1,500 kilometres, in a single day.

13

TIME TO TAKE YOUR TEMPERATURE

Weather-watch for 30 years and you'll discover the climate. *Climate is what you expect; weather is what you get.*

Near the Equator, there are two seasons; wet or dry and temperatures and climates stay more-or-less constant.

Further north and south, there are four seasons: spring, summer, autumn and winter. In these regions, temperatures and weather change, according to the sun's position. Days are short and cold in winter, whilst summer brings long, warm days. It's all because the Earth tilts!

The Earth orbits the sun. At different times of the year, one part of the Earth is tilted more towards the sun – making it summer; whilst the opposite end is pointed away from the sun – so it's winter.

The northern and southern hemispheres have reverse seasons at the same time! When it's cold, wet and wintry in Europe, China and the United States, it will be hot and summery in Australia, South America and South Africa.

MEET THE NEIGHBOURS

Did you know that the driest and one of the wettest places in the world are next door to each other?

In South America, the rain that falls on the eastern side of the Andes flows into the world's largest river - the Amazon. To the west, the same mountain range prevents the Atacama Desert in Chile from receiving any rainfall; making it the driest desert in the world.

If the rain keeps up, there'll be a drought.

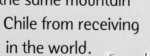

WHERE TO GO TO FRY AN EGG

The **Sun's** temperature averages 5,700°C. *Your egg would be toast.*

The closest planet to the Sun, **Mercury**, has a range from minus 180°C to 400°C… *the mercury is rising.*

On **Venus** temperatures heat up enough to melt lead, 465°C.

At lunch-time on the **Moon**, temperatures reach 107°C - hot enough to boil water without fire. At night though, minus 153°C, *brrrrr…*

Mars, *where I'm from, it's a beautiful* minus 63°C to 20°C… *you'll need a jumper if you come and visit.*

Jupiter, Saturn, Uranus & Neptune, it's cold or very cold: minus 150°C to minus 214°C.

Pluto, even colder at minus 378°C, *we think…*

PRAY... WHEN WILL IT RAIN?

Weather worship has been a part of life for 1,000s of years. Early civilisations believed that the weather was controlled by the gods. If angered, these gods could call up devastating disasters like droughts or floods.

Early weather experts were witch-doctors, tribal elders or priests. There were no weather channels, maps or satellites to forecast the weather. Instead, prayers and gifts were offered up to the gods.

Some weather experts have more hidden talents than others

In times of drought, it was thought that rain-dancing might please the gods and bring rain – a tradition still practised in some places today.

Are you a weather watcher?

Can you look at the sunset, sniff the air, feel the breeze, or watch animals and insects to predict tomorrow's weather?

Do you know why cows lie down in fields when it rains?

Many people believe that the full and new moons bring weather changes. *Do you?*

A SECOND FULL MOON IN A MONTH IS CALLED A 'BLUE MOON'

Who are the Weather Gods?

In Ancient Egypt 5,000 years ago, the ruling Pharaohs were believed to be descendants of Ra, the sun-god, who rode on the moon, with the sun on his head.

3,000 years later, Apollo and Helios, the Greek and Roman sun-gods, rode across the sky in fiery chariots.

Early Northern Europeans worshipped Thor, the Norse god of thunder. He carried a huge hammer representing a thunderbolt.

700 years ago, the Central American Aztecs, believed Tonatiu, their sun-god, controlled the weather.

Today in China, dragons are thought to be the rulers of water and the weather.

In native American mythology, the thunderbird creates thunder, lightning and rain.

On the Pacific island of Tonga, the king is said to be a direct descendant of the sky god.

TODAY'S FORECAST

Meet Weather-Pod. Hooked into the grid, he has downloaded some serious answers.

For instance, what's the study of weather called? *Meteorology* - from the Greek word *meteoron*, meaning something that happens high in the sky.

More than 2,000 years ago, the Ancient Greeks looked to the skies and tried to understand how the wind, rain and clouds were connected.

Aristotle, a great thinker and writer lived in Greece, around 340 B.C. His book, *Meteorologica*, was the first major study of weather. His best friend, *Py-storm-front-ius* thought that a *red sky at night was a great delight*, but Aristotle didn't believe anything could be that simple.

Weather is all about how big your front is! Less than 100 years ago, physicists worked out the importance of the huge cold and warm air masses and the 'fronts' where they meet.

Today radars, satellites and high-performance aircraft probe storms and monitor major weather systems. Super-computers collect massive amounts of data; from the size of raindrops to giant storm activity.

People who study the weather are called meteorologists. They have the best jobs. Some chase giant tornadoes in trucks. Others fly around studying clouds.

Of course… you could pop your head out of the window to check the weather, but if you want to look after it, it's good to know what it's up to!

If you're chasing a storm, be prepared to come second

CLOUD SEEDING

At weather school, there are many classes but my favourite is how to grow things.

Have you heard of cloud seeding? *No... it's not gardening.*

If the weather conditions are right, you can sow the clouds and reap rain!

Cloud-seeding planes fly high up, looking for suitable cloud-banks in which to sprinkle very tiny amounts of chemicals such as silver iodide. This chemical freezes the moisture in the clouds. When the small ice crystals grow and join together, they get heavy and fall as either rain or snow... *sometimes even in the right place!*

Got green thumbs? Try your hand at cloud-seeding

How BIG is the weather?

The **World Meteorological Organisation**, set up by the United Nations in 1951 has over 185 member countries, all providing data on world-wide weather observations.

Data is collected from 11,000 land stations, polar orbiting satellites, radar stations, 3,000 aircraft, 7,000 ships and oil rigs.

All this data is sent to world weather centres to be analysed by super computers.

Four times a day, atmospheric measurements are recorded on land and sea by the **World Weather Watch** (WWW) - a global meteorological system.

The oceans temperatures are being measured by floating robots!
The ARGO project involves 60 countries and nearly 2,000 high-tech robots which float one kilometre below the ocean's surface, measuring the heat content. This data is used to help predict global weather patterns.

WHAT'S ON THE MENU?

Rain-clouds are billions of tiny drops of moisture floating around in the air. They bump into each other, join up, grow big and heavy and fall as rain or snow. Clouds form when air is cooled to the point where the moisture in the air becomes visible. This temperature is called the dew-point.

Thunderstorms are storms that can drop millions of litres of water and release more electricity than is used in a large city over an entire week. Thunder is the sound that very hot lightning charges make.

Lightning is a giant spark of electricity, hotter than the surface of the sun. Lightning is attracted to the ground. You can tell how close lightning is, by counting the seconds between seeing the lightning and hearing the thunder. If you are really close, you'll see the flash and hear thunder immediately, as one sharp crack.

Rainbows are created when sunlight passes through raindrops. A rainbow has all the colours of the spectrum, but usually you only see seven: red, orange, yellow, green, blue, indigo and violet. To see a rainbow, the sun needs to be behind you. Have you ever seen a double rainbow? *That's something very special.*

Snow is made from tiny crystals of frozen water. Lots of ice crystals join together and form snowflakes. Snowflakes have no colour - they reflect light so the colour appears white. No two snowflakes are the same.

A **cold front** is the front edge of a cold mass of air. On a weather map, the triangular points face the direction that the cold air is moving towards. A **warm front** is the front edge of a relatively warmer mass of air. The rounded half-moon shapes on a weather map face the way that the warmer air is moving towards.

Tornadoes form over land and are some of the most destructive spinning wind-storms on earth.

Tropical Cyclones are warm windy storm systems that have different names depending on where they appear. **Hurricanes** are giant storms that form over the Atlantic Ocean. **Typhoons** form in the Pacific Ocean. **A tropical storm** is one that forms over a warm ocean. It can strengthen and turn into a hurricane or typhoon.

Take a Deep Breath The amount of carbon dioxide taken out of the atmosphere by plants each spring is almost perfectly balanced by the amount put back into the atmosphere in the autumn. It's as if the planet takes a huge breath in and out, each year.

EXTRA DISHES...

POO-looter is desperate for a holiday, but he's out of luck. He has been given all this extra nasty pollution to get off the ground. Pollution brings its own, very special kind of weather, especially created - by you.

SMOG – is a mixture of smoke and fog produced by industry, motor vehicles, incinerators and open burning. Smog hangs around over densely populated cities, for example, Los Angeles, Mexico City, Athens, Beijing and Hong Kong.

ACID RAIN – pollution emitted by power stations, factory emissions and motor vehicles. Mixed with rain, the acidity of this pollution destroys forests, eats away buildings and poisons water and soil.

AIR POLLUTION – car exhausts emit carbon monoxide and coal burning produces sulphur dioxide: two examples of very harmful air pollution.

DUST STORMS – large areas of cut-down forests and bare agricultural soil are great sources for dust storms. When the wind blows, tonnes of dust get kicked up into the air.

TURN DOWN THE SUN

Recently the amount of sunlight reaching Earth has dimmed. Called Global Dimming, it is caused by an increase in air-pollution and longer-lasting clouds.
Who turned out the lights?

Poor Poo-looter... he would so like to have a holiday.

TODAY'S WEATHER: BALANCING THE BOOKS

If you are looking for a great place to live – you can't go past planet Earth. With a superb selection of weather, temperatures and climates, there's something for the whole family! If you visit Venus, you'd burn your bumps off, *(it gets so hot)* and if you were marooned on Mars, you'd freeze your freckles off - it's so cold there.

Earth is such a pleasant place to live, thanks to a great gang of gases, known as the **Greenhouse Gases**. Their job is to keep the temperature, not too hot or too cold – perfect for life.

After the sun's rays hit the Earth, some beams are reflected back towards outer space. On their way, they are held up by the GHG gang, which grab the sun's reflected infra-red heat and stop it escaping the atmosphere.

Thanks to those captured sun-beams, Earth's average temperature is kept at a liveable level - around 15°C. Without the GHG gang, Earth's temperature would be about minus 18°C - too cold for life. *Take it from a Martian… we know these things.*

However, things are changing. Right now your planet is getting all steamed up. Put simply… world-wide, it's getting hotter.

Would you like chips with your planet?

STAND AND DELIVER

It was less than 200 years ago that electricity lit the first light bulb. Since then, the world's population has quadrupled. Now there are over 6.5 billion people - and rising. They all want to use power for light, heating, cooking and transport.

Why is the planet heating up?

Everyone uses energy. Mostly, this energy comes from fossil fuels - coal, gas and oil. When fossil fuels burn, they release billions of tonnes of extra greenhouse gases. If enough of these gases are set free, the thin layer that already exists in the atmosphere starts to thicken, preventing more of the sun's heat from escaping. *It's like adding blankets.*

When the sun's rays can't get away, the GHG gang, gang-up on planet Earth and turn up the heat.

Climates have changed many times through the Ages. The study of ice cores, fossils and pollen, prove there have been at least four global freezes. Volcanic eruptions, the shifting of the earth's plates, a wobble in the planet's spin, solar spots and meteors hitting the Earth, all can contribute to either an ice age or global warming.

When things get tough, try not to be a sun-beam

WHY IS IT DIFFERENT THIS TIME?

If scientists are right about Earth's projected temperature rises over the next 100 years, temperatures are rising faster now than at any other time in the last million years.

I'm sure people don't mean to heat things up but for the first time in planetary history, science shows that human activity is making the climate change.

Want to meet the people responsible for turning up the heat? It could be... YOU.

MEET THE GHG GANG... ALSO KNOWN AS THE BIG 6

Carbon Dioxide has been passing gas for over 4 billion years. Once there was 80% CO_2 in the atmosphere but today there is a tiny 0.038%. Without it, Earth would be frozen.

Atmospheric CO_2 comes from the decay of plants, volcanic eruptions and no... *don't hold your breath....* all animals exhale it when they breathe out.

Chlorofluorocarbons (CFCs) have no natural source; they are produced entirely by human activity. CFCs were used as refrigerants in air conditioners, refrigerators, freezers, and heat pumps. Even though CFC production has been vastly reduced, they will remain in the atmosphere for along time.

CO_2 is chemically stable in the atmosphere and can last about 100 years. It's removed from the atmosphere by plants and can dissolve into water, especially on the surface of oceans.

On Earth, carbon is found in all organic material - in oceans, rocks, soil, plants, animals and of course, underground in fossil fuels.

CO_2 is now, at its highest level for 650,000 years. Almost 27,000 million tonnes of CO_2 are released per year world-wide. *What is everyone doing to create all this GAS?*

Nitrous Oxide (N_2O) is also known as laughing gas.

Released by burning fossil fuels, the use of certain fertilisers and industry.

It is rare... 1,000 times more rare than CO_2 but one molecule is around 200 to 300 times more effective at trapping heat.

Ozone (O_3). The presence of Ozone in the stratosphere is a good thing, but the presence of Ozone in the troposphere, is a bad thing. *How confusing.*

Since the Industrial Revolution, the level of Methane in the atmosphere has almost tripled. 600 million tonnes are released each year from landfill, waste treatment and cows' bottom burps!!

In the troposphere, Ozone is a major element of urban smog, damaging crops and enhancing the greenhouse effect.

Methane (CH_4). Generated naturally by bacteria that break down organic matter. Found in the guts of termites and other animals and in natural gas deposits. Known as marsh gas: it's commonly seen bubbling up from marshlands.

Huge reservoirs of natural Methane are stored under the surface of the oceans. Methane is 21 times more powerful than CO_2 at storing heat.

Water Vapour – the most common Greenhouse Gas. A small increase in global temperature would lead to a rise in global water vapour levels.

DOING THE SUMS

The Greenhouse Gas gang live naturally in the atmosphere. Now, humans are sending extra numbers of them up: turning up the heat and causing weather changes. Do the sums - even if you are a brilliant mathematician, it doesn't add up.

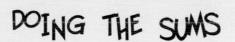

HOW DO YOU COOK A PLANET?

Each year, billions of tonnes of fossil fuels - coal, oil and natural gas - are mined and extracted from under the Earth's surface; providing energy needed for homes, industry and transport.

Energy runs the modern world. Most energy comes from burning fossil fuels. Fossil or carbon-based fuels are made from stored sunshine, captured by vegetation from the days of the dinosaurs. More than 200 million years ago, as plants and animals died, they were buried under mud which gradually hardened into rock. The rotting plants and decaying animals were squashed and heated by the earth. Over millions of years they changed into coal, oil and natural gas deposits.

Why is fossil fuel so popular? It's easy! You can just dig it up; it burns quickly and produces power that's very easy-to-use.

Over the last 200 years so much fossil fuel has been burnt or 'combusted' that now there is 25% more CO_2 in the atmosphere. *You try doing your work with all that extra gas around.*

These extra gases or emissions are called 'Enhanced Greenhouse Gases'. They might seem friendly enough but they are unbalancing the natural 'Greenhouse Gas' gang.

CHEAP POWER

China and India are home to one in three of the planet's population. Both countries have large reserves of fossil fuel and huge numbers of people living in poverty, without decent food or shelter.

By 2020 China will have built more than 500 new coal-fired power stations. India will be close behind.

In these countries, fossil fuel is the easiest way to build up industry, in the hope that one day these populations can enjoy a similar life-style to other nations.

Imagine all the natural Greenhouse Gases happily sitting on a see-saw. When the Enhanced Gases want to join in, the balance is upset.

How do you cook up a planet? Release 45 billion tonnes of extra Greenhouse Gases into the atmosphere each year and wait. It will keep getting hotter!!

Balance is an important part of life

WHAT'S FOR DINNER?

There's a global warning out.

Each time you turn on a light, open the fridge or put fuel in your car, you are probably adding to climate change.

The problem has been made worse because billions of trees which, in the past, helped to absorb CO_2, have been cut down for timber and to make room for farming.

Fossil fuel is used everyday, in hundreds of ways.

What did you have for dinner?

Where did the food come from?

How is it kept fresh?

A truck would have transported your food along with many other boxes of goods to the supermarket. They all need fossil fuel energy to be made or kept fresh.

How does the fridge stay cold?

How much energy is needed to package your food?

Does your car run on fossil fuel?

How do the lights and air-conditioning stay on at the supermarket, your school and at your house?

Where does all the energy come from?

Fossil fuel is even used to make frozen peas! The peas may be picked by hand, but they are trucked, *fossil fuel drives the truck*, to a refrigerating unit, *which runs on fossil fuel*: packed in materials, *created using fossil fuel energy* and kept frozen *in freezers that use fossil fuel power to stay chilled.*

THE WEATHER MONSTERS

It's official. A group of scientists called the **Intergovernmental Panel on Climate Change** says that temperatures will probably rise between 1.8°C and 4°C within the next 100 years.

This might not sound much but even one or two degrees can massively change the weather. Warmer temperatures heat up the oceans and unbalance the moisture in the atmosphere, creating extra heatwaves, storms, floods, fires and droughts.

Climate can only bend so far before it snaps and changes for good. Pump enough greenhouse gas into the sky and the last part behaves like the last degree when you boil a kettle, turning hot water into sizzling steam. Melt enough ice at the North and South poles and suddenly whole glaciers will break-off into the sea.

WEATHER IS NOT AN EXTREME SPORT

As the temperatures climb, seas expand and water levels rise.

44% of the world's population, (more people than inhabited the entire planet in 1950), live within 150 kilometres the coast. *How close to the coast are you?*

If sea-levels rise as predicted, 200 million people will become homeless.

11 of the warmest years on record occurred between 1995-2006.

Global warming also causes regional cooling by slowing down ocean heat transport.

50 million people each year, already deal with record-breaking floods caused by huge hurricanes and storm surges. *You could become one of them.*

Unless, temperatures stop rising, half the land surface of the Earth will be drought-affected by the end of this century.

Warmer water temperatures act like rocket fuel for typhoons and hurricanes. Category 4 and 5 storms have doubled in the last 30 years, while wind speeds and the duration of hurricanes have increased 50%.

FUELLING THE WEATHER

Look around you. Nature has had enough.

Melting glaciers and polar ice caps are increasing the risk of flooding and threatening the lives of penguins, polar bears and seal colonies. More than 20% of the North Pole Ice Cap has melted away in the last 25 years.

Lakes and rivers are freezing later and thawing earlier each year, disrupting the life cycles of native plants and animals.

Coral reefs and the life they support are dying, as their homes get too warm.

Seasons are shifting. Spring comes earlier and autumn lasts longer.

Ecological glitches occur and food patterns are becoming mis-matched. Species are starving or becoming extinct.

Higher temperatures cause plants and soils to soak up less carbon from the atmosphere. They also thaw the permafrost, potentially releasing large quantities of methane.

Ecosystems are particularly vulnerable to climate change. One study estimates that around 15–40% of species face extinction with an increase in temperature of just 2°C.

Bushfires are increasing. Forests that don't go up in smoke are moving uphill as tree lines try to escape the heat and drought of the lowlands.

The economic cost of global warming and its effects are estimated in trillions - more than the combined cost of the two World Wars and the Great Depression. This is equal to a fifth of the global economy but that's nothing, it could cost the Earth if left too long.

CLEAN GREEN ENERGY

The Stone Age did not finish because people ran out of stones – it ended when people decided that iron was a better material to use. In the same way, the fossil fuel age will not end when people run out of fossil fuels. It will end when enough people stop using fossils fuels and choose to use more sustainable energies.

That choice is already available. Sustainable or renewable energy - green energy, is clean energy; available from sources such as the sunshine, wind, flowing water and waves. It can even be captured from the heat of the earth's core – geothermal energy.

What does all this type of energy have in common? *Let me count...*

It won't upset the weather;

It won't harm the environment;

It does not contribute to global warming;

It will not increase the risk of floods or fires and

It will not melt the ice caps or

threaten extinction for 10,000,000,000s of animals, insects, bugs and plants.

Green is clean and fossils are mean.

So far, green energy has not been adopted on a large scale. Most countries think it is too expensive to use while there are still large reserves of fossil fuels in the ground. Within the next 50 years, we believe they will change their minds.

Clean energy is just around the corner

HARNESS THE WEATHER

Green, clean energy is out there and it's free.

Chill out time. Choose to use renewable energy and give the GHG gang some space. Then the planet can re-balance the weather - naturally.

Catch the Water - Running water is one of the most widely used forms of renewable energy. Hydro-electric power is created by passing water through turbines which drive generators to produce electricity. 20% of the world's electricity is produced in this way. Iceland, Norway, Austria, Canada and Tasmania produce most of their electricity from harnessing the power of water.

Capture the Wind - Wind power is now a very competitive renewable energy source in windy parts of the world. Denmark has around 6,000 huge wind turbines that supply 20% of the country's total electrical power. Germany and Spain also use wind power to create electricity. Globally, wind power generation quadrupled between 1999 and 2005 as costs dropped by 80%.

Trap the Sun - Another great energy source; on clear days, solar energy can replace the billions of barrels of fossil fuel oil that currently go up in smoke. Buildings can be designed so that sunlight powers the air-conditioning and heating.

Boats, buses and even cars can run on solar power. Up in space, sunlight is converted to electricity by solar panels and is used to power satellites and the space station.

Scientists have worked out that the whole world's demand for electricity could be met today, by covering a 600 square kilometre area of the Sahara desert with solar cell technology.

These are some of the alternate, eco-friendly sources of power and energy on offer. They won't get the planet all heated up and won't upset the weather.

Surf the Wave. Around 75% of the earth's surface is covered in water and every wave that crashes to shore contains energy. It's limitless, free and clean: a real alternative to fossil fuel energy in the future.

YOU HAVE THE POWER...

You can help to stop the planet from overheating, reduce fossil fuel emissions and cool things down by being energy-efficient: it's very simple

Kidz Power. Be a nag... tell your family, friends and everyone you know that green is clean and fossils are mean.

Drive a new breed. If your family buys a car, help them choose a fuel efficient one. Hybrid cars use a mixture of technologies and can cut fuel emissions by 70%.

Use both sides. Reduce paper waste. Don't use six sheets of toilet paper when two will do! It takes less energy to make recycled paper and will slow down the destruction of the planet's great forests.

Plant trees. They absorb CO_2 and give off oxygen.

Fresh is best. Frozen food takes 10 times more energy to produce. Avoid packaged foods. Cut down your rubbish and you'll reduce GHG emissions.

Be house proud. If you install solar hot water and power systems - the sun will give you energy for free.

Turn it off. Is your electricity bill the same as last year? How can you make it lower? Turn off the lights when you leave the room as well as the T.V and computer; rather than leaving them on stand by.

Lighten up. Use energy efficient light bulbs, shower heads and white goods. Shut the fridge door. Let food cool down fully before putting it in the fridge or freezer.

Give fresh air a work-out. Hang clothes out to dry rather than putting them in a tumble dryer.

Call a Greenie. See if there is a green power option. It just takes one phone call.

Are you an Environmental Hero? Encourage your family to apply for the renewable energy rebates on offer. If enough people use green power, hybrid cars, energy-efficient fridges and solar panels, prices will drop. This will encourage more sales and help countries like India and China to afford clean power.

PLANTING THE SEEDS OF CHANGE

There are changes in the air. Don't be square... look out there. it's not a dare... NOW is the climate for change.

Take a bus and plant a tree. Greenhouse neutral buses operate where some bus companies plant trees to balance the fossil fuel emissions produced. Bio-diesel buses can also replace traditional buses.

Invest in Green. China will spend $200 billion on renewable energy over the next 15 years. Their goal is that by 2010, a tenth of their energy will come from environmentally-friendly sources.

Bank your credit. Put a price on pollution. Europe and Asia already have a programme for trading carbon and other heat-trapping gases. Companies calculate their contribution to carbon emissions and trade by buying or selling their credits and debits.

Catch the Gas. Methane, a major GHG contributor, is a natural by-product of the decomposing organic matter that is disposed of in landfills. If captured, it can be converted into energy.

Use the Sink. Carbon sinks are underground reservoirs where captured CO_2 can be deposited. Natural sinks are forests and oceans. Some governments are looking at drilling holes and injecting the CO_2 under the ground and into the ocean floor.

See the Light. Australia is following the lead set by Cuba to phase out conventional light bulbs and replace them with energy-saving globes that use only 20% of the electricity needed to produce the same amount of light.

Hungry microbes. The munching microbe is back! Scientists have uncovered breeds of methane-gobbling microbes that love munching methane emitted from mud volcanoes. *For them it's like chocolate cake.*

Inventions. Car numbers in the world will double to 1.2 billion, within 20 years. Hydrogen cars may be part of the solution. Honda and Toyota and other car manufacturers, are producing more fuel efficient cars.

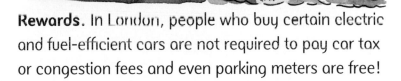

Rewards. In London, people who buy certain electric and fuel-efficient cars are not required to pay car tax or congestion fees and even parking meters are free!

Choice. In California, builders offer home-buyers roofing tiles that convert sunlight into electricity.

PROOF IN THE PUDDING

Need proof that you can change weather patterns?
Look up – it's happening right above you.

Ozone gas is one of the natural GHG gang.
It has been protecting life on this planet
from the sun's harmful rays for billions
of years.

In the 1980s scientists discovered
that a large hole had opened in the
Ozone layer, mainly over Antarctica.
It was caused by the release of artificial
chemicals from aerosol cans and sprays.

Alarmed governments signed an international treaty,
called the *Montreal Protocol,* to ban ozone-destroying
gases such as CFCs, found in aerosol cans and
air-conditioners.

By 2006, scientists agreed that the Ozone hole over
Antarctica was shrinking and could close completely
within 50 years. The ban on chemicals that had
thinned Earth's protective film of gas was showing
signs of success.

If it's possible to help close a hole that is 15 kilometres
thick and more than 29 million square kilometres large,
it should be a doddle for you to tackle the problem
of climate change.

Always keep a sewing kit handy

The Kyoto Protocol
The Kyoto Protocol is the only International Treaty created to fight climate change. After a
heated debate, the participating countries signed up to reduce six key greenhouse gases.
International commitment by all nations is needed to adequately reduce global Greenhouse
Gas levels. A tougher treaty is already being discussed.

IF YOU WANT FINE WEATHER... MAKE IT YOURSELF

It's no good burying your head in the sand... the weather and the planet's thermostat are in your hands.

Doing nothing is no longer an option. Just a small difference in what you do can make the world of difference. You have the power to control the weather, the climate and the temperature and your planet is depending on you.

Everyone loves to talk about the weather, so now talk about it until everyone listens.

Global warming can be stopped. NOW is the climate for change. There's enough technology today to set this planet free from the evil clutches of fossil fuel.

Lay it out to play it out... it won't cost the Earth to save it.

We believe in making it happen.

Working together will harness the weather.

Come on, get mean... go green... you've got a planet to save...